2

Can't Raise No Man

Katandra Jackson Nunnally

Printed in the United States of America

Cover design by Elaina Lee
Edit by Danielle Bell

First Printing, 2015
ISBN 978-0-9861001-3-0

FreedomInk Publishing
P O Box 1093 Reidsville, Georgia 30453
www.freedomink365.com

1. Family & Relationships : Parenting - Single Parent

2. Social Science : Statistics

3. Biography & Autobiography : Personal Memoirs

Dedication

I dedicate this book to the single parents out there that have either by force or by choice, raised children on their own. Please take comfort in knowing that you are not alone.

I dedicate this book to every woman that has had to defend her parenting style and/or relationship status as a counter to the misconception that 'A woman can't raise no man!'

I dedicate this book to my son. Jermaine Trevon, I do believe that you turned out alright. I did alright. We did good kid…

Special thanks to a very special group of Ladies that took it upon themselves to support this book before it went to print. I appreciate your support as I continue this literary endeavor. I just want the world to read. Thanks y'all for believing in me.

Renae Laurent Jackson

Alena Brewton Smiley

Yvette Porter Moore

Shanika Lawson Smith

Evelina Holmes Cooper

Can't Raise No Man

Katandra Jackson Nunnally

First comes the baby in a baby carriage...

Oh to hell with love & marriage. I'm a married woman NOW sure enough. But my new status in life has not always been the case. I've had my unfair share of days of being husbandless. Left to rear children on my own, alone. No decent male role model around long enough to even be considered for the role of stepfather. Each application was denied before any even bothered to fill one out. And they never did. Stick around long enough that is.

Just a list of unimportant individuals whose names I've since forgotten. Boyfriend after boyfriend. All of them boys and all of them commitmentphobes! Each one bearing his own brand of fear. Fear of staying. Fear of being responsible. Fear of becoming a man. So I raised him on my own, alone!

Would you please quit sangin' that same old sad damn song...

"Oh you're just a woman."

"You can't raise no man."

"He need a daddy."

"Honey, where yo' husband at?"

Every great aunt had that look in their eyes. Thank heavens the generations before mine believed in getting married and staying married. Even if the wife was a miserable wreck and all the husband did was cause her grief with every child that was born outside of their marriage! Well now where is the 'Happily Ever After' in that? So keep giving me them side eyes and on occasion ask the question, but would you please quit sangin' that same damn song? I've heard it all before. "You can't raise no man!" The path I saw his father heading down was making a pretty bold statement of its own. That's when I made the decision that, "Yes. You're going to have to raise this [man] child on your own!" Even before his lengthy departure, I was preparing to go it all alone.

And baby makes two...

A certain bond is created once a woman knows that she is carrying life. That bond solidifies and becomes more concrete when she feels that very life for the first time. A lucky hand may on occasion feel the bumping around. Even an eye or two may claim witness to this miracle. But it is nothing like experiencing this life from the inside. No two human beings can have a closer connection than when a mother is expecting! She has been chosen and she knows it. The Universe knows it. Every hand feeling, every eye seeing. They all know. It's just them in their own little world. Mommy, and baby makes two.

"No matter who decides to come and go, it's just me and you kiddo! Who are they to tell me that I can't raise no man? We'll show them."

I'm not certain the exact percentage of the population that grew up without a constant father figure in their lives. In my world, the majority of us were raised without a dad. Single mommas, occasionally aunts rising to the challenge of raising nieces and nephews. And Grandmothers, the ultimate matriarch of most families. After her own children are grown and gone, she continues to fulfill a civic duty as the head of her ancestral household.

Where I'm from, most fathers are gone long before we graduate from high school. Who am I kidding? Most fathers leave somewhere between the time right before we are born, to our very first day of school. Perhaps that's just the way it is in my little world!

Then there are those that have been fooled by the disillusioned mirage of a dual parent household. Mother and father. From the outside looking in, it all seems quaint. However standing in the midst of the family unit, it's clearly evident that although two parents reside within the home, only one rules supreme when it comes to raising the children. And in my world, where I'm from, that reigning parent is usually the Mother! Do not, I repeat, DO NOT BE FOOLED!

I tried. He tried. We tried...

"Mama's baby. Daddy's maybe." These infamous words became the undercurrent of my parenting style. I'll be blunt and absolutely transparent about the situation! My son's father did not stay. I tried. He tried. We tried. Not in vain but to no avail. Too many slights administered to one another during the early days of a budding relationship, dab smack amidst the seedling phase of our youth. But every rose, in its own season will bloom, smell as sweet, whither, die and decay into the Earth beneath. So was the case with our love. The evidence that remains is our son. My first born.

This is by no means a baby daddy bashing book. But you can't have the child without the father. With that said...

He and I met one fateful evening. I was in middle school and he was in high school. He was popular. The star Running back of the football team. He played basketball. He ran track. He was Mr. All-American. About as good looking as they come for one born and raised in a small town in the south. Tall, light skinned with dimples any girl could just drown in. And when he smiled, the corners of his eyes would squinch and crinkle just so. Pearly white teeth and chiseled muscles. The right words just seemed to always be spilling from those pink lips. Yeah... He was good looking alright!

Did I like him? If I had eyes that could see, I did! He was something else. But life had other plans. My family moved from Georgia to Florida and I lost all contact with this 'Teenage God'. When Fate makes up her mind that "Well dear, this is just the way it's gonna be." she does not take mercy on the brokenhearted.

Circumstances brought my family right back to my birth state and wouldn't you know it, directly to the small town he called home! It didn't take long for our paths to cross once more. This time I was a little older, but not much wiser. I was still naïve. My sophomore year of high school was his first year out of school. "Oh look at me. Dating an older man. You little girls ain't got nothing on me." I didn't openly voice it, but secretly I mocked them all.

My mother wasn't exactly thrilled about the relationship. Here I was still pretty fresh in the world, just learning who I am and I go and hook up with a guy that is older than me, out of school, has his own car... And a job. Of course back then I had no idea what credentials a man should be ready to present. But in my eyes he had so much going for himself, how could he not be a keeper. Then of course it didn't hurt that he was just so darn good looking!

I was a stubborn, headstrong, stupid girl. If there was something that my mother ever objected to, I'd dig my heels in and have my way just for the hell of it. Oh baby did I have my way. She'd say no and I'd sneak out...

Or sneak him in. I guess after a while she decided "If you can't beat em, join em." So now the rebellious wild child had permission to openly date Mr. Gorgeous. Let's talk about sex! I suppose it goes without saying that we were doing it. A lot! I'll spare these pages the details of the whens and the wheres and the how oftens... Like I said, it was a lot!

Young, naïve and not yet pregnant, I was learning all about love. It was certainly too late to have that talk about the birds and the bees! Not only had he and I done the deed, but we had done so repeatedly, without an ounce of afterthought of what the repercussions would entail. I was his girl and in order to remain in those good graces, I was constantly tested. I was supposed to act and react a certain way. If I loved him... I was supposed to look and not look a certain way... If I loved him. I was supposed to do certain things... You know the rest. And I did. Foolishly but never regretfully.

I know you're only 16, but...

Not long after that first hookup did I feel a change in my body. My breasts hurt, I'd get sick at the smell of food, my period stopped coming. A few weeks before my 17th birthday I received the news. Compliments of the local county Health Department.

"I know you're only 16, but if you love me, you'll have my baby!"

Oh baby was I in trouble!

The same day that I found out, my mother announced that she's a mind reader, clairvoyant, all knowing of every little secret that teenage girls keep. After that Nurse announced, "You're pregnant" with a look that screamed, I don't know if I should congratulate you on the life that is growing inside of you, or chide you for being such a stupid little girl, still a child yourself; my first thought was of my mother. Without fail I'd imagined at least a dozen different ways that she'd kill me once she found out. The thing is, I never told her. She told me. Just kind of spit it out when she came home from work that same day. She stood there in the doorway with her purse half hanging from her left shoulder, hand still on the knob as if for support. Her right hand sitting squarely on her hip, fingers digging into her flesh, a futile attempt to keep from putting those hands around my scrawny neck. She stood there, every bit the tired single momma and all thoughts of Mr. Good Looking flew out the window. She stood there. Looking at me and then she said it. "You pregnant ain't you?" I couldn't even muster up the courage of a new mommy in defense of this helpless life. Couldn't even breathe a simple "Yes ma'am." So I just nodded and thought to myself, "Oh baby, am I in trouble now!"

I was verbally assaulted by a myriad assortment of choice words. I never knew my mother's vocabulary could be so vivid, her language so colorful. But if ever there were at least a thousand ways to tell your teenage daughter what a fool she was to allow herself to get into such a predicament, well, I heard em' all on that day. I knew that I had screwed up royally.

Being the older sibling, I was a good big sister and experienced babysitter. But babysitting a little brother and caring for my own baby are certainly not created equal.

I had no idea what I'd gotten myself into but somewhere in between my mother's deservingly livid rant, I distinctly heard her say, "This is your baby, you alone will raise it." The words that kept reverberating in my ears like some lunatic echo were 'your' meaning all mine, nobody else's responsibility and 'alone'...

We've all heard the expression, "You've made your bed. Now you have to sleep in it." My version of it goes a little something like this, "You rolled around in a perfectly good bed. Now look at the mess you've made. Go on. Sleep in that messy bed!"

Goodbye high school and hello real world.

"Having a baby don't make you grown but you will be taking care of this responsibility on your own, alone!

I'll provide the roof over your head. I'll make sure you eat. But I ain't changing no diapers. I'm not getting up in the wee hours of the morn. I'm not wiping so much as the first snotty nose. And babysitting? Forget about it!"

Okay, so it wasn't that bad, but the implied threat that I'd be sleeping in that messy bed that I made was aptly and abundantly applied. I got the message loud and clear. With my mother working hard to maintain the home that just grew by one, thanks to my doing, I knew that I'd be leaving my friends soon. It was Goodbye high school and hello real world.

My junior year of high school was my last. There'd be no Homecoming, no Prom, no Senior Ditch Day, no Senior pictures, no Grad Night, no walking across the stage, no class ring, no cap and gown, no diploma. There'd be no High School Reunion for the teenage dropout. A few of my classmates were expecting as well. I think there was something amiss in the water that year. I think most of them returned to finish their senior year and graduate from high school. I was forced to stay at home and raise my first born.

You must have been a beautiful baby... You must have been a beautiful child.

And he was. A beautiful, bouncing baby boy who entered this world, fatherless. That word 'alone' came back to haunt me on the day of his birth. My son's father had long since quit his job and began getting into trouble that he'd soon have to pay for. I'm told that at the exact time my son slipped from my body into this world, when he took his first breath, the time recorded on his birth certificate as time of birth, it is the exact same time that his father was being placed in the back of a patrol car, driven to the county jail to be booked for a crime. Talk about Fate and her ill-timed sense of humor.

If memory serves me right, our son was a full month old before his father laid eyes on him for the first time. During visitation hours, for 20 minutes, through a dirty, scratched up plexi-glass, 10 x 10 inch square carved out of a steel door that was supposed to be the equivalent of a window. Welcome to the World little guy. Your daddy loves you so much.

Well kid, it's just me and you. What's next?

At the young age of 17, I had no idea what to do with a baby. I mean, c'mon let's be real. Having a baby doesn't automatically qualify you as being an adult and the reality of it is, I was still a baby myself. "Well kid, it's just me and you. What's next?"

You join the league of ever growing statistics, that's what's next. You drop out of school. You stay home. You take care of your responsibility. You sleep in that messy bed. This is not the way I envisioned my life. I was supposed to graduate from high school, with honors. Apply to and attend a top University and again, graduate with honors. Move into the workforce. Adopt an amazing career. Fall in love. Get married. Have babies. I suppose I was too impatient to go the route that I initially intended. I skipped straight to the 'Have babies' part. Genius plan!

My senior year of high school, I spent at home with my son. My mother never missed a day of work. I had her love and support sure, but the little guy was my sole responsibility. My mother was still taking care of her own children. A brother, 5 years younger, as well as an unruly teenager. I was in no way prepared to be in the world on my own. I was still in need of her care.

While my friends were enjoying our, their, final year of high school, making memories, going to dances and attending Prom, I was learning how to be a mommy. Snotty noses, dirty diapers, formula, pacifiers, late nights, early mornings, colic, ear infections, and the crying. Dear Lord, Jesus Christ up above, I never knew such a little thing could make such a big fuss. And the tears. Mine and his flowed like the Euphrates. I was raising my first born as I struggled to grow up myself.

Disclaimer: I dropped out of high school to raise my son. However, I did return to the educational arena a few years later. Obtaining my GED as well as an accredited Diploma from a local technical community college. I would go on to apply to and be accepted into Georgia Southern University. Although my degree in Psychology is temporarily on pause, it has not been forgotten. I digress... The point of this disclaimer is to say, the road became much harder to travel with a baby in tow. The best method to ward off an unwanted teenage pregnancy and possibly becoming a high school dropout, is to practice abstinence. Yes, that means no sex! Now back to the story already in progress...

The years they did come and go. Some, more quiet than others and some, marking dates and incidents on my forever timeline.

I can't recall the exact year, but I remember the holiday well. It was Thanksgiving, I remember a younger cousin making a very accurate remark. "You and Tre aren't like mother and son. You're like sister and brother." The observation was a true but simple statement, still it pained me to my core. I've jumped a few years ahead of myself. Back to the first few years of his life...

He was a sweet baby. A little slow to hold his head up, roll over, crawl and walk. Just as slow to hold his own bottle. He seemed to cry for no apparent reason. Like some invisible ailment had a vice grip on his little body. That little face with its scrunched up nose, almond shaped eyes, pouty pink lips and those cheeks! Oh so kissable. I loved to kiss my baby boy. And he obviously adored his mommy! Even if I did feel like a failure. All I saw when I looked into his eyes was unconditional love!

A few years passed by and lo and behold, some girls just never learn. I once again fell under the hypnotic spell of my firstborn's father. We were dating again. We were doing it again. We, well rather, I, got pregnant again. A few months before our second child was born, this time a daughter, I found out that my sweet baby boy's iron level was unusually low. The local Health Department scheduled an appointment for my son to be checked out by a specialty doctor. We traveled an hour from my small hometown to Savannah to be seen by a Hematologist/Oncologist.

I was clueless as to what this doctor was going to tell me. A mother's worst nightmare confirmed is to know that her child is sick and it is somehow her fault. My son was 3 years old, I was a few months away from giving birth to his sister and I heard those words for the very first time. The words that shook my world and forever changed the course of mine and his life and possibly even the child that I carried inside of me.

"Ms. Jackson. Your son has sickle cell disease."

What is sickle cell disease? How did my son get it? Why am I just finding out? What does this mean for my son? Will it affect my daughter?

Sickle Cell Disease is an ailment of the blood. It is a disease that affects primarily, but not exclusively, those of African descent. Healthy red blood cells travel through the body, round and flexible, happily with ease. Sickled blood cells are riddled with an abnormal hemoglobin which causes the cells to mutate into a 'sickle' or 'V' shape. They travel though the body not so happily, getting stuck along the way and causing excruciating pain in the joints, limbs and larger extremities! From my understanding, it's believed the roots of Sickle Cell Disease can be traced back to Africa and the widespread plague of malaria. The body found a way to stave off one disease and in doing so another took its place. The genetic mutation is either passed from one parent that has the disease or both parents that have the trait. The percentage of which children will be born with the disease is anybody's guess. {For more accurate and in depth information about Sickle Cell Disease, please visit www.sicklecelldisease.org}

The hospital my son was born at wasn't required to include Sickle Cell Disease screening during newborn testing. So it went undetected in his poor little helpless body for years.

The disease is inherited. It is one that will be with my child for a lifetime. It's only known cure is a bone marrow transplant and only fatally ill patients are candidates as the procedure itself can be extremely risky. Seeing as how the same mother and father that produced the first child, got together to procreate once more, we'd have to play the waiting game to see if baby number two also had this disease. My son will be taking antibiotics and pain medications for the rest of his life. Heavens above... I'm the worst parent on this earth.

"Baby boy, momma is so very sorry. I'm going to find a way to make it up to you. I promise."

That first appointment was a blur. My son was sick. He always has been. His days as a baby came back to haunt me. All the crying. All those times he looked like he was in so much pain. He was truly hurting. I never even knew.

I took it upon myself to learn as much as I could about Sickle Cell Disease. I asked the doctors a million questions. I kept track of everything they told me. I wrote down every appointment and the name of each medication my son was prescribed. I researched everything I could get my hands on. By the time my first born was ready to enter elementary, I knew which pain medications worked best and which he was allergic to. I understood the dynamics of his ailment. But the one thing I refused to do was to let this disease ruin us. I believe that every sickness is 10% physical, 90% mental. I know that physically speaking, those sickled cells are running rampant through my son's body just waiting to wreak havoc. His grandmothers were all too willing to coddle the child. And much too ready to chastise me for not being a bit softer with him.

Have you ever heard the term, 'Tough Love'?

He was my first born. He received the very essence of tough love. I knew in my heart that if I treated him in a manner as to say, "Oh you poor baby. My poor child. My son is sick." I knew that if I approached raising him post diagnosis, in that manner, that the percentages would flip. The disease would become 90% physical and 10% mental. I was not about to let anything, especially not some medical prognosis, determine our happiness.

Sickle Cell Disease became my son's silent brother. We knew that he was always in the room but we refused to acknowledge him. We went on about our everyday lives as if this sickness were not a part of his body. The only time that we did accept this truth was when my son would become too ill to remain at home.

That silent brother can be such a beast at times. Lying dormant for weeks, months, years at a time and then out of nowhere the agonizing pain. Joints and limbs. Hands and feet. The worst, head and chest! Sickle Cell Crisis is what these pain episodes are called. Before he celebrated his 10th birthday, my son had already had his gall bladder removed, a spleen sequestration, one blood transfusion and he'd been hospitalized at least a dozen times. Each time we checked in at the hospital, we hunkered down and prepared for a 2 week stay.

I was a novice pro by this time. I knew the doctors, the medicines and the medical jargon. I'd kept my son in the loop from day one, explaining to him in a manner that he'd understand just what was going on. Even when he was very small he could tell you what type of Sickle Cell Disease he has, which medicines he is allergic to and which work best for pain.

Being without a significant other in my life, I had to ensure that my son could be my eyes and ears and my mouth as well if I needed to step away from his sick bed. And often I did. My son is the eldest of 3 siblings. Just because sometimes he is not well does not mean that everything screeches to a halt. No! Life goes on. The girls have school, they have homework, and they must be fed and bathed and lovingly put to bed so that each new day can begin again. How else could I be in two places at the same time other than to make all parties aware? That meant I was responsible for letting the Nurse in charge of each night's shift know that I was just a phone call away. I'd leave my number on the table near my son so that he could call if there was an emergency. I would then say a prayer that all that is well, remains well and that the next day will be even better than the day before. The best defense we had in our arsenal was knowledge. Knowing that God is in total control and knowing that my son knows his condition just as well as I. Truth is, the older he gets, he may know even more than I do. I'm okay with that.

The hardest day ever did not involve any pain associated with Sickle Cell Disease. It was the beast itself and the indirect, unforeseen hurts that reared its ugly head. My son was very much interested in sports just as his father before him. He had for several years played football for the city's Recreation Department. He was a member of the Pee Wee League and then the Junior League. I never gave it much thought, I just supposed that because he was young a physical was irrelevant. Any child that wanted to play, played. This love of sports carried on with my son beyond the age maximum allowed to play with the Recreation Department and eventually he was too old to play with those teams. So he set his sights on middle school sports. I foolishly hoped for the best when he brought home the form which stated that a physical was required, mandatory to even be considered. This form had to be filled out by a Physician before my son would be allowed to tryout!

In my mind the whole idea of following through with the physical seemed absurd. I doubted any doctor would give him the green light to play. But in my heart, I hoped that I was wrong. My son was ever optimistic. We had asked the 'special' doctors repeatedly during numerous check-ups, if he'd be allowed to play school sports. The doctors told us that the decision would be at the discretion of whatever doctor performed the physical. We took the drive after school one day. I paid the fee. The Physician said... "No."

My sweet son was crushed. He cried inconsolable tears. There was nothing I nor any doctor could do to make the pain go away. All he wanted to do was play and that was taken away from him. The seriousness of this disease dawned on us in a new light. The Physician that performed the physical decided upon a 'no' due to the fact that the older my son got, the rougher the sport would become. Football was no longer child's play. It was a big boy game. A tackle from my son's peers whom were physically larger than my son during his early years, could trigger a pain crisis and the episode could be detrimental.

Football was no longer a part of our lives. We were down but certainly not out. Too much harsh physical contact you say? How about baseball?

And he excelled at this new game. Thank the heavens that not every athletic avenue was stripped away from him. He played baseball and eventually we would encounter a JROTC Sergeant who understood my son's condition and offered to be an extended part of his circle of Caretakers, remembering not to push him to the point of exhaustion, allowing constant hydration and keeping extra watch when his shift was in full swing.

That all important circle of Caretakers wasn't envisioned with the inclusion of girls. But as life goes, my son was growing up and maturing and girls were a new interest that I wished would remain some foreign, less understood affair. So much for wishing he could just stay a little boy. The appearance of these little women got me to really thinking about my son's future. Who will take care of him in his adult years and what about children of his own? The fact that he has Sickle Cell Disease, heightens the chances of his children being born into the same unfortunate fate.

You have a child. African American. Male. Born to a teenage dropout. Raised by an on-again, off-again single mother. Minus the presence of a full time father. Plus a lifelong disease that he may potentially pass to a child of his own. My heart often hurts for him. Why won't life just give him a break?

But that's just it. Life is meant to define character. Either the adversities we face will break us down or build us up. We are the determining factor. We decide how we will respond to the hardships.

My firstborn and only son has had quite the life thus far. Too many Dr's to name and too many hospital stays to number. He's had a spleen sequestration, a blood transfusion and his gall bladder was removed, all before he reached his teenage years. We've prayed our way through blood clots. A moment I may remember for the rest of my life is my son, looking up into my face with tears in his eyes saying, "Thank you Mama." Clearly in pain, but thankful that I, his mother, found the courage to give him medication via injection in his abdomen, for days on end. What he doesn't know is that I'm not as brave as he thinks. I'm not so sure I could have endured even a fraction of what he's faced in his young life.

The journey ain't over yet. We've come a long way and my son has finally got the hang of managing pain at home. That means lesser hospital visits unless the pain becomes too unbearable and self-medication, rest and hydration at home aren't relieving the crisis. There are still many miles to go.

Don't be mistaken. My son is not around the clock sickly. Oftentimes I forget that he even has this disease. And Lord knows, he ain't a saint. That boy has given me plenty of mama grief and heartache. He's no angel. He's fallen in with the wrong crowd. Has had an unlikely brush with the law. He's come home once, so drunk, he could barely stand. I've recently discovered tattoos that he didn't have parental permission to go out and get. And if I discover one more discarded condom wrapper, I'm going to lose my entire mind. Overall the [man] child loves to remind me on a daily basis of my own wild and crazy and over rebellious teenage days.

At the completion of this book, my son is 17. He along with his sisters and myself, have welcomed into our foursome, a permanent fixture, my new husband and the children's stepfather. My son will be 18 in a few short months and it seems that the most important phase of his rearing has already been done. But it's never too late to step in and give a hand and that is just where his stepfather has entered our lives. To love and cherish not just me, but my children, our children, as well.

They say that there is no way that a woman alone, can raise a man. I say, what situation is absolutely perfect? I did my very best. I had the love and support of family. My son has had the guidance of uncles and grandfathers and on rare occasion, male role models such as his prior JROTC Sergeant. Then there are those ex-boyfriends that will remain unnamed, that I kept company with for a short while and during their temporary tenure, they too taught important lessons along the way, like how to ride a bike and how to tie a tie.

Life is about living and learning and sometimes, life is about making mistakes! Was it a mistake to have a baby when I was still a child myself? Was it a mistake to walk away from relationships that could have at least secured the presence of a father figure in his life at an early age? Will my son suffer because he wasn't raised in a two parent household? Is his destination damned as a man because he was raised by a woman? Perhaps. Or perhaps, life will test us despite our upbringing and early family life. Perhaps it doesn't matter who raises a child; mom, dad, mom and dad, grandparents or some other familial or unrelated legal guardian. Perhaps instead, what matters the most is HOW that child is raised and what each child chooses to do with that upbringing. And when you raise a child to the best of your ability, with the help that is provided, all the love you can muster, a little luck and God lighting the path, perhaps after all, a woman can't raise no man... But a village can!

ABOUT THE AUTHOR

Katandra Jackson Nunnally is the CEO of FreedomInk Publishing. She spends her time delicately balancing the role of that responsibility alongside the continuous pursuit of being an Author.

The CEO/Author resides in South East Georgia, where she shares a home with her children Jermaine Trevon, Kailyn Elise and Ashley Vanique, three pups, Liberty Rebel, Boss & Bentley, and her husband, Jeremy!

Formerly Ms. Jackson, Katandra Jackson Nunnally is an avid Reader, sporadic Tweeter and aspiring Instagram junkie, who's totally obsessed with Facebook. Social media rules!

In the midst of her online presence, Mrs. Nunnally is also a pretty darn good chef, chauffeur, referee, stiletto addict, Poet, Blogger, Mojo replenisher, Carnal Sobriety redeemer, and raiser of men!

Connect with 'Kat' at FreedomInk.
www.freedomink365.com/about_the_publisher

Check out these amazing books by the Author!

The Bride Diaries (The Diary of A Bride To Be Books 1, 2 & 3) is the literary romantic comedy about one girl's determination to earn the bling, wear the white dress and walk down that ever elusive aisle. She is determined to claim her version of heaven on earth. Wedded bliss will be hers even if she has to sneak up on it unsuspecting from the shadows of like, lust, love, bop it over the head, stun it into silence and carry it off, too dazed to resist, to the land of Happily Ever After! The series is funny, quirky, zany, happy, sad, full of triumphs and life's little upsets.

Ladies, are you subscribed to The Bride Diaries? Guys this book is for you too!

All FreedomInk Publishing books are available at Amazon, Barnes and Noble, Books-A-Million, and anywhere amazing books are sold.

FreedomInk Publishing. Books that entertain, educate, embolden, empower & enlighten...

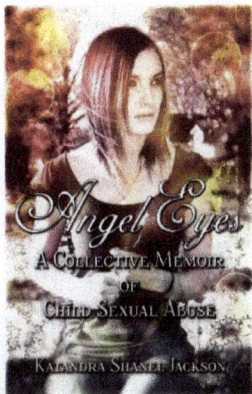

"Angel Eyes: A Collective Memoir of Child Sexual Abuse, rips open and tears down the veil of child sexual abuse, revealing the rawness of this crime against the innocent. This is not a book for the weak at heart... As you will definitely cry, and at the very least be affected. It is a book that everyone should read none-the-less, because when a people are ignorant and have a lack of understanding, we will perish and we allow this preventable disease to corrupt and grow, being passed down to our next generation..."

~Yvette Porter Moore
(San Diego, California)
Founder of Root Digger Genealogy

*Please contact the Publishers' home site for an autographed copy of Angel Eyes.
www.freedomink365.com

Or contact the CEO/Author directly at
freedomink@yahoo.com

Or purchase direct via this link...
http://bit.ly/1pb6BoZ

Carnal Sobriety...

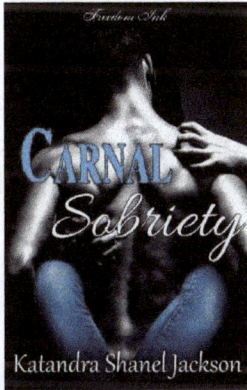

Monday through Friday. Weekends. Yes Saturdays and Sundays too. No day was holy. Sex became my religion. I sacrificed my soul for those Earth shattering minutes. Every day I locked myself away from the world. My goal? An orgasm at any cost. My vibrator was my best friend. It knew what I needed. It was what I needed. My dependency grew so strong that it became near impossible to reach climax with a temporary lover...

We all need inspiration, motivation and encouragement from time to time, but where can we turn to find it? Mojo For Sale: the Art of Encouraging One's Self, highlights a wealth of sources that are easily within our reach. This little book of encouragement packs a really big punch and is ready to serve as your guide to the inspiration within.

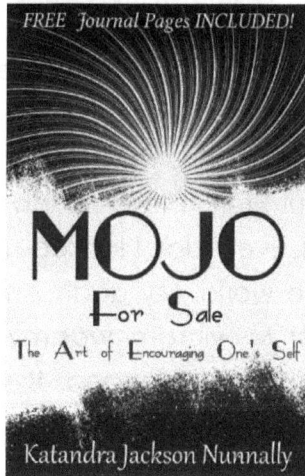

FREE Journal Pages INCLUDED!

MOJO
For Sale
The Art of Encouraging One's Self

Katandra Jackson Nunnally

Keep reading!

www.ingramcontent.com/pod-product-compliance
Lightning Source LLC
Chambersburg PA
CBHW060422050426
42449CB00009B/2085

* 9 7 8 0 9 8 6 1 0 0 1 3 0 *